Catch
the Anointing

DAG HEWARD-MILLS

Parchment House

Unless otherwise stated, all Scripture quotations are taken from the King James Version of the Bible.

CATCH THE ANOINTING

1-1 Extract from *A Passion For The Gospel* by Colin Whittaker. Used by permission of Kingsway Publications, Lathbridge Drove, Eastbourne, BN23 6NT

2-2 Extracts from *Understanding the Anointing* by Kenneth Hagin. Used by permission of Faith Library Publications & Kenneth Hagin Ministries Inc.

3-3 Extracts from *All Things are Possible* by David Edwin Harrell Jnr. Used by Permission of Indiana University Press

4-4 Extracts from *The Release of Power* by Bishop David A. Oyedepo. Used by permission of Dominion Publishing House

5-5 Extracts from *Tragedy Trauma Triumph - WHY?* by T.L. Osborne. Used by permission of OSFO International

Copyright © 2000 Dag Heward-Mills

First published by Parchment House 2000
Published by Lux Verbi.BM (Pty) Ltd. 2008
Published by Parchment House 2011

Published by Parchment House 2013
25th Printing 2019

ISBN: 978-9988-596-00-2

[77]Find out more about Dag Heward-Mills at:
Healing Jesus Campaign
Write to: evangelist@daghewardmills.org
Website: www.daghewardmills.org
Facebook: Dag Heward-Mills
Twitter: @EvangelistDag

Dedication
I dedicate this book to ***Bishop Nicholas Duncan-Williams.***
Thank you for paving the way for the church in Ghana.

Contents

1. You Must Be Anointed 1
2. Associating with Great Men of God.............................3
3. The Art of Soaking in Tapes 7
4. My Testimony..13
5. Catch an Anointing..19
6. The Art of Preaching and the Anointing.....................22
7. "Aman" and "Tsalach" 28
8. Six Giants Catch the Anointing 34
9. Why Some People Never Catch the Anointing 49

CHAPTER 1

You Must Be Anointed

I had no formal training in the ministry; no Bible school and very little contact with any great man of God. When I started out in ministry, some of the men of God I came into contact with, ended up doubting and fighting the call of God on my life. I had no option but to tap into the anointing that was on other more distant men of God through their tapes and books.

I believe that I am anointed with the Holy Ghost to stand in my office of ministry. I have too much evidence around me to doubt the reality of the anointing on my life. I also believe that the electronic and technological development in the world is for the benefit of the kingdom of God and the ministry. Technology has made it possible to get close to people who are anointed.

It Is the Anointing That You Need

When God sends you a man of God, you are given a chance to receive him and catch the anointing that is on his life. The anointing is the principal thing that you and I need to do God's work.

The prophet Zechariah knew that the most important thing was the anointing. It was he who said, "Not by might, not by power, but by my Spirit" (Zechariah 4:6).

Elisha also realized that the thing which made Elijah's ministry successful was the anointing. When he had the opportunity, he asked for the anointing. Some people may have asked for the money, the education or the qualifications that Elijah had. But Elisha just wanted the anointing!

...Elijah said unto Elisha, Ask what I shall do for thee, before I be taken away from thee. And Elisha said, I pray thee, let a double portion of thy spirit be upon me.

2 Kings 2:9

In this book, I want to share about *a channel of anointing* that is not usually spoken of. It may sound new to you, but it is very real. If there is any way by which you can catch the anointing, please take it! I am not presenting this as the only way that God can anoint you; I am only sharing with you what I have received from the Lord. I am sharing with you what is biblically and scripturally sound.

Many people have received the anointing through listening to tapes and reading books, but they do not understand what has happened to them. **Many of those who have received the anointing through this channel cannot teach it because they do not fully understand it**. I believe that it is my duty to teach this simple and real method of catching te most essential ingredient of ministry - *the anointing*.

CHAPTER 2

Associating with Great Men of God

In another book[1], I have shared about the importance of associating closely with the man of God in order to receive the anointing on his life. Why do you have to associate with anointed men of God? What exactly do you acquire through association? As you closely associate with a man of God, you will hear him speaking over and over again. These words contain the anointing. When Elisha associated himself closely with Elijah he heard him speaking over and over again.

And it came to pass, as they still went on, and talked...

2 Kings 2:11

Words Are Powerful!

Jesus told his disciples that his words contained two important things. They contained life and the Spirit! What is this Spirit? The Spirit is the anointing! The Scripture says that God anointed Jesus of Nazareth with the Holy Ghost and with power (Acts 10:38).

Jesus was anointed with the Holy Ghost, and therefore the Holy Ghost (the substance with which he was anointed) is the anointing.

...the words that I speak unto you, they are spirit, and they are life.

John 6:63

For many people, the close association with men of God we speak about is not possible except through the medium of books and tapes. Books and tapes may contain the words of anointed men of God. The words of anointed men of God contain the Spirit and life.

"Soaking" in books written by anointed men is an invaluable way of associating with them. The time you spend reading a book is spent fellowshipping with the author of the book. What a great privilege it is to interact with a great person for three hours in the privacy of your home!

As you read this book you are fellowshipping with me and I am fellowshipping with you. As I write this book, I feel that I am talking to certain people. I am ministering directly to as many as would take the time to receive. Just as Elisha listened to the words of Elijah and the disciples listened to the words of Jesus, you are listening to my words as you read this book! The disciples listened to the words of Jesus, that is how they were anointed.

You can be with Jesus today by reading his words in the Bible. I am constantly amazed at the number of ministers who do not read the Bible. They just use the Bible as a tool for preaching. The Word of God is, first of all, for your benefit.

You will not be a minister of substance if you do not have your own personal fellowship with the Lord. I do not mean a last-minute check of certain Scriptures before you preach. A quick check of a Scripture is different from fellowshipping with somebody through the written Word. Fellowship with

Jesus everyday. God wants to interact with you. He wants to fellowship with you. God's desire since the days of Adam has been to fellowship with man.

When Moses came down from the mountain after fellowshipping with the Lord, the glory of the Lord was upon him. The glory of the Lord will be upon you when you fellowship with God.

When I woke up in this world, I found myself in Ghana, West Africa. I realized that I was very far from the great men of God in America. I desperately wanted to fellowship with them but there was no way possible. I did not even have a visa to America, nor had I any money to buy a plane ticket. Even if I had been able to get there, many would have seen me as a crazy black man who was trying to get too close! They would have called their security guards to protect them from me. So God showed me a way that I could fellowship with some of the most anointed people of this generation; their books and tapes!

I have fellowshipped with many people through their books. I got to know their minds through their books. In the same way, I have interacted with the Lord Jesus by reading the Bible and studying his words and actions.

One of my favourite portions of the Bible is the Gospels. In the gospels (Matthew, Mark, Luke and John), I can see what Jesus said and I can hear him speaking to me personally.

The anointing makes people take notice of you.

...and they took knowledge of them, that they had been with Jesus.

Acts 4:13

Two Types of Receivers

There are two types of people who may receive the anointing – those who are physically near and those who are physically afar off. You see, some people have the opportunity to be physically near to the anointed vessel. The Apostles, Peter, James and John were physically close to the Lord. They touched him, they held him and they even had dinner with him. This is their testimony:

That which was from the beginning, which we have heard, which we have seen with our eyes, which we have looked upon, and our hands have handled...

1 John 1:1

Unfortunately, Apostle Paul did not have the chance to physically interact with Christ as the other apostles did. Paul was just like me, he had to depend on books! He loved his books. That is why he sent urgently for his books and parchments (booklets). He had to study and fellowship with the Lord and other great men of God like Isaiah through the written Word.

The cloke that I left at Troas with Carpus, when thou comest, bring with thee, and the books, but especially the parchments.

2 Timothy 4:13

If Paul had lived in our generation he would have used all the technology available to receive even more of the Word and the anointing. Paul would have listened to tapes and watched videos. **Books contain the written Word, but tapes contain the spoken Word**. You can catch the anointing from the spoken Word.

---

[1] *See The Mega Church by Dag Heward-Mills*

CHAPTER 3

The Art of Soaking in Tapes

Soaking in the messages from tapes is a scriptural practice. "Soaking" in tapes simply means to listen to the words over and over again until it becomes a part of you and until the anointing passes on to you! When a tape is fully "*soaked*", both the Word content and the Spirit content are imbibed into your spirit. **The anointing is not something you learn, it is something you catch**.

Do not assume that the "soaking" in of the tape is just an educational exercise. It is a spiritual event. Two important things happen when you soak in a tape. First, faith comes by hearing, and hearing by the Word (Romans 10:17). Secondly, the anointing of the Spirit through the words, comes into you.

The Spirit enters a person as he receives the Word of God. That is why many people experience a radical transformation by just listening to a powerful message from the Word of God. That is how come people are saved when they hear the preaching of the Word of God. The Holy Spirit enters into them as the preaching goes forth and they are born again.

The Bible says that we are born of the Spirit.

That which is born of the flesh is flesh; and that which is born of the Spirit is spirit.

John 3:6

Being born again is not an educational experience. Being born again does not mean that you have learnt something new. It means that a spiritual change has taken place. Your spirit has been recreated by the Holy Spirit. This experience of being born again, completely and forever changes a person's life. It happens when people listen to the preaching of the Word of God. That is why we invite people to church. We want them to be exposed to the preaching.

In the same way that when you are born again, you experience a spiritual transformation, you can also experience a further spiritual transformation that will convert you into a minister. This spiritual transformation that makes you a minister is what some call "*receiving an anointing*" or "*being anointed*". There are too many people who are called ministers, yet they have neither received a call to ministry nor the anointing to minister.

When you have not been anointed, you are dry and lifeless. I used to go to church every Sunday and I hated it! It was a lifeless and boring experience. I only went because my parents had asked me to go. Unfortunately, not only are some so-called ministers not anointed but they are not even born again. This is even worse! You do not become a minister by obtaining a certificate. **You become a minister when God calls you and anoints you**!

Churches do not grow because there is no anointing for church growth. Pastors everywhere must desire the anointing. It is the anointing that makes the difference! Once you know the anointing, you will not want anything else. You will not succeed in the ministry by being clever. Intelligence and education are not substitutes for the anointing! Desire the anointing! Go for it! It is the main thing! And the main thing is still the main thing!

Jesus' First Sermon

The first sermon that Jesus preached was about the anointing. The first thing that he said when he began his ministry was that he was anointed.

The Spirit of the Lord is upon me, because he hath anointed me to preach the gospel to the poor...

Luke 4:18

In fact, Jesus did not attempt any form of ministry until he was anointed. Jesus knew that the ministry depended on the anointing.

Church Elders

I recently visited a large beautiful church. The pastor himself was not around so the janitor took us around the building. The main hall had hundreds of beautiful mahogany pews. It was a beautiful building with two huge pipe organs and surrounding balconies.

I asked the janitor, "How many people does this building seat?"

He answered, "This building seats at least eight hundred and eighty people."

"Wow," I remarked, "That's a lot of people!"

He continued, "But, we don't have many people coming to church anymore."

"I see. How many people come to church nowadays?" I asked inquisitively.

"About twenty, with a maximum of thirty people." He added, "Only old people attend church now. The young people don't come to church anymore."

I thought, "How sad. Such a large church has been reduced to a fellowship of twenty old and dying people."

Obviously there was no life. But that was not all. The janitor continued, "From this month onwards, the services are being held every two weeks instead of every week."

I thought to myself, "We hold church services on almost everyday of the week. There is so much life in our church. It is full of mainly young people who want to serve the Lord. What a contrast!"

The difference between a growing and a dead church is the anointing. The anointing is the life of God in the ministry. Oh, how we need the anointing! We cannot do without the Holy Spirit.

So how do we come by this Holy Spirit? That is what this book is about. God is trying to show you that you need the anointing. You may be ministering the Word. You may even be ordained. However, it is only when you are anointed that your ministry will begin to make a difference to the lost masses of humanity. I see the anointing on you right now as you read this book!

The prophet Ezekiel experienced the anointing entering his life one day. He described exactly how and when the anointing came upon him. Ezekiel sensed that the power and the anointing of the Spirit had entered into him whilst he was listening to the Word.

And the spirit entered into me when he spake unto me...

Ezekiel 2:2

Ezekiel said very clearly in this scripture that the Holy Spirit entered into him when he was being spoken to.

Peter, the apostle, also noticed this phenomenon. He noticed that the power of the Holy Spirit fell on people as he preached. Do you remember when Peter was preaching to the Gentiles? The Bible says that as he ministered the Word, the Spirit of God fell on the people.

While Peter yet spake these words, the Holy Ghost fell on all them which heard the word.

Acts 10:44

If the gift of the Holy Spirit could fall on people whilst Peter was preaching, then surely the gift of the Holy Spirit can fall on you when any other anointed man of God is preaching. This is simple logic.

How It All Began...

At five o'clock in the morning on January 1st 1987, I decided to obey the call of God on my life. It was in the early hours of the first day of that New Year when I decided to take up the mantle and become a pastor. I knew that I had been called, so I had decided to obey and become a pastor.

At the time, I was in the fourth year of medical school. I began the church with a few nursing and laboratory students in the Korle-Bu Teaching Hospital, where I was studying medicine. I had no one to direct or guide me so I struggled quite a bit during that first year.

By the end of 1987, many friends had expressed their lack of confidence in me and deserted me. I was criticized until I felt like killing myself, just to make my enemies happy. I remember looking at the ceiling fan as it twirled above my bed. I often thought of hanging myself on it. I wanted to vanish out of the view of all those who hated and criticized me. I had very little guidance, but I was sincere and had a lot of faith, and many enemies. It is amazing how people hate you when you decide to follow the call of God.

This was the precarious and doubtful beginning of my ministry. I started out by faith and began teaching and preaching what I knew. A few nursing students responded.

In the beginning, the church met in a little classroom at the School of Hygiene. After a while, many people left and some stayed. The little church stabilized with about forty members. But something happened to me in 1988 that made a big difference to my ministry. It transformed the ministry from a little classroom full of nursing students to a ministry that impacts thousands of people around the world today.

CHAPTER 4

My Testimony

S ometime during the middle of the year 1988, I had to fulfil what is called a "Community Health Rotation". Every class in medical school is divided into groups. Each group rotates through different fields of medicine throughout the year. That is why it is called a rotation. I had to complete four rotations in my final year: surgery, medicine, specials and community health.

During the Community Health Rotation, I had to travel outside the city of Accra to a smaller town called Suhum, in another region of the country. While I was there, I lived in the Suhum Government Hospital for one month. I was there to gain practical experience in running a hospital and working out on the field where conditions are different from the bigger cities.

Although I was fulfilling my medical requirements, as usual my mind was on the ministry. By the second week, I took advantage of a more relaxed timetable and decided to fast and pray. On my way out of Accra to Suhum, I had passed through a Christian bookshop and bought some of Kenneth Hagin is tapes.

I felt that I just needed something to soak in whilst I was in Suhum. I had been a great follower and admirer of Kenneth Hagin's ministry. Actually, I had already listened to those particular tapes many times before, but I just wanted to have something to listen to. No one had ever told me to listen to tapes. I just enjoyed doing it. I loved the Word and I loved the minister of the Word. No one had ever told me to listen to tapes over and over. I was not trying to memorize the message although I ended up remembering almost every sentence. Listening to tapes never replaced my Bible study and personal quiet times. I was not losing my personality! I wasn't becoming a clone. I was being blessed tremendously!

One night I was praying, fasting and listening to one of the tapes that I had bought. I remember that day as if it was yesterday. I was using a small red auto-reverse tape recorder. The message that was being played was about dealing with demons. It was a message I had enjoyed listening to many times. The tape played non-stop throughout the night.

Something Happened!

At about 3 a.m., I was kneeling by the bed praying. I could see the tape recorder situated at the other end of the room. Then suddenly, something literally jumped out of the tape which was playing and moved into my belly. I could feel it entering me. Then I heard a voice saying, "From now you can teach." I did not know what that was but I thought to myself, "That is good, because I want to teach." **I did not know at that time that I had received a major impartation of anointing through the** *channel of soaking in tapes.*

At that time, my church comprised about forty students. The Bible teaches that we should prove all things, so I decided to try out this new gifting. I was invited to teach at a Full Gospel Businessmen's breakfast meeting in Suhum. This was the first ministration after my impartation experience. I tell you, I noticed a difference.

After the ministration, someone asked me where my church was. He was surprised that I was an unknown minister. Inside me I knew that something had happened that was making a difference.

When I got back to the church, after a month's absence, I noticed a difference in my ability to teach and preach. The anointing had arrived and I began to build up. The first series I preached was about the prodigal son. I preached this series during our weekday services. I soon noticed that the attendance and interest in the service began to increase steadily. I tell you, I noticed there was some life and Spirit in the ministry.

It is difficult to describe it but when it is there you know it is there! The anointing is a bit like beauty – when you see it, you know it! You cannot easily explain how or why you recognize beauty. But when you see beauty, you know that it is there, and so it is with the anointing!

I have no reason to give for what I am sharing except to help you. My ministry has grown in leaps and bounds because of the anointing I caught from soaking in the Word on a tape. Today, you are reading one of the several books that I have written under that same teaching anointing.

At that time, I did not have any biblical basis for what I had experienced, so I did not talk about it. Later, as I studied the Word of God, I realized that the mystery of impartation of anointing through the soaking of the Word is a reality. It is biblical! It is doctrinally sound and it is experimentally real!

Anyone who exposes himself to "soaking in" the Word through books and tapes is exposing himself to more of the anointing! When you do that, only good things will happen to you.

On different occasions I have heard people describe how they have received the anointing as they sat in the congregation and received the ministry of the Word.

One pastor described how he felt warm drops of anointing falling on his head as I spoke the Word at a Camp Meeting. I believe the Lord was anointing this man.

T. L. Osborne, the great evangelist, described how God changed his ministry as he sat under the ministry of William Branham. It all happened in a moment, and then he was anointed to go out and be a great witness to the world. It is interesting that outsiders sometimes are better receivers than insiders. Do you remember the story of the centurion whose servant was sick? He sent for Jesus because he knew that Jesus had the anointing and power to heal.

And a certain centurion's servant, who was dear unto him, was sick, and ready to die.

And when he heard of Jesus, he sent unto him the elders of the Jews, beseeching him that he would come and heal his servant.

And when they came to Jesus, they besought him instantly, saying, That he was worthy for whom he should do this: For he loveth our nation, and he hath built us a synagogue.

Then Jesus went with them. And when he was now not far from the house, the centurion sent friends to him, saying unto him, Lord, trouble not thyself: for I am not worthy that thou shouldest enter under my roof:

Wherefore neither thought I myself worthy to come unto thee: but say in a word, and my servant shall be healed.

Luke 7:2-7

This man realized that there was anointing in the words of Jesus. So he sent another message to Jesus.

He said, "Don't bother to come all the way here. Just stand there and say something."

In other words, "There is no need for you to even lay hands or pour oil on my servant, just speak some words and the healing anointing will flow."

He sent his word, and healed them, and delivered them from their destructions.

Psalm 107:20

The Angel Appears

One night, whilst ministering at a Miracle Wave Convention, something astonishing happened. There were thousands of people present that night and the power of God was "flowing". That night I remember that when I finished preaching the Word, I felt that God had already moved. It was not even necessary to do anything further. There was a lady sitting up in the balcony with her baby and husband.

This lady suddenly experienced an open vision. Her eyes opened supernaturally and she could see me and everybody else on the stage. But she also saw a huge angel standing on my left hand side suspended in midair.

She said, "As you were preaching, you would say things like, 'I see you blessed!', 'I see God answering your prayer!', 'I see you healed in the name of Jesus!', 'I see you owning a car!'" She said the angel would hand out blessings as I spoke and smaller angels would carry them to the people.

She said that some people had outstretched hands and were very receptive. The angels would go straight to them with the blessings. Whilst others were receiving, others were dozing off and missing out on the spiritual impartation that was taking place.

I believe that this angel goes around with me whenever I minister. I know that that "big guy" has been assigned to me. He is my ministering angel.

Spiritual things are as real as physical things. The Bible teaches us that angels are ministering spirits that minister for us. They work for us and help us. That is why the angel was distributing spiritual parcels to those who were receiving the Word.

Are they not all ministering spirits, sent forth to minister for them who shall be heirs of salvation?
Hebrews 1:14

CHAPTER 5

Catch an Anointing

Anyone who listens to tapes and reads books will receive to a greater or lesser extent some anointing. Some people are not impressed or moved by the message. Some are even offended by it. As Jesus said, "Blessed is he that is not offended in me." Some people are excited by the message. Some cannot remember anything, they just know that it was a good message.

As you listen to a tape, you learn the message. You learn the Word. You acquire the knowledge content. Some people stop at this point. But others go even further. I went further without even knowing what I was doing. Somehow it was not the knowledge content that I was after. If it was knowledge, I had virtually assimilated all the facts that were being shared after a few times of listening to the tape. My love for the Word made me expose myself to the anointing without even knowing it.

I remember being blessed by the messages of a pastor of a huge church in Los Angeles, California. I had a few videos of his that I thoroughly enjoyed. I would watch these videos over and over again.

As I watched this pastor preaching in his church, I desired to have a church like that and to preach as well as he did. One day, I was preaching in my church, walking up and down the aisle when the Spirit of God told me, "This is it!"

It suddenly dawned on me that I was walking in the steps of the pastor that I had watched and listened to for years. I was teaching and preaching like he did. I was pastoring a church which was as large as I had seen on the video tape. You see, when the anointing is on you, you will do certain specific things in your ministry.

Do you want to have a big church? Catch the anointing that is on someone who has a big church. Do you want to be an evangelist? Look around and see who God is using and follow that person. Listen to his tapes and read his books. The anointing will fall on you one day.

The Specificity of the Anointing

The anointing is like your gun. It does certain specific things. You just have to use it and direct it where you want to. Every anointing has a way of working itself out to achieve specific results. The anointing that was on Elijah made him do certain things.

Do you want to be a teacher of the Word? Then follow someone who has a teaching anointing. The anointing is very specific. The healing anointing is different from the teaching anointing which is also different from the pastoral anointing.

Elijah miraculously caused three years of drought. He multiplied the meal and oil of a widow, caused the resurrection of a young boy and called fire from Heaven. Elisha did similar things. He also caused years of drought, performed healings, and multiplied a widow's oil. It is interesting to note that Elisha did exactly twice as many miracles as Elijah did. Elijah did sixteen miracles and Elisha did thirty-two miracles! Elisha had a double portion of Elijah's anointing.

The anointing is a very specific substance that makes you achieve certain things. **You can desire a specific minister's anointing**. God may have put it in your heart to achieve certain things in the ministry. Elisha went for Elijah's anointing without any apologies to anyone.

If you catch the anointing which is on certain person, you will do similar things because it is the same anointing.

John the Baptist also carried Elijah's anointing. There were many similarities between the ministry of John the Baptist and Elijah's ministry. Both of them had dramatic ministries and both of them confronted kings. Both of these men were familiar with deserts and solitude. They wore the same type of garments and lived simply. Both of them had their ministries terminated by queens.

Benefit from the Tapes

In order to gain the maximum benefit from a tape, you must listen to it with a vision of eventually receiving an impartation of the anointing. Listen to the same tape several times. In my experience, this is different from listening to many different tapes of the same minister. When you want to get to Level F, as described in the next chapter, stay with the tapes you enjoy. Listen to tapes unconsciously and listen to them whilst praying and fasting. Allow yourself to receive the gift of God that is ministering to you. You must be open to the man of God who is ministering. You must receive him with admiration and with love, otherwise, you will get nothing from him or through him.

But as many as received him, to them gave he power...

John 1:12

21

CHAPTER 6

The Art of Preaching and the Anointing

You can learn how to preach and teach by listening to tapes. I have not been to Bible school and did not have the privilege of being taught how to deliver a sermon. But there are many ways of learning the same thing.

When I was practising medicine, I learnt a little phrase from the surgical department. The phrase is, "Watch one, assist one and do one." What does this mean? It means that if you want to learn how to perform surgery, you watch one operation, assist one, and then you actually attempt one yourself.

Everyone can learn how to preach by listening to preaching. In fact, the best thing you can do is to listen to other ministers all the time. The prophet Daniel studied what the prophet Jeremiah had taught. The prophet Jeremiah ministered from 685-616 B.C. and the prophet Daniel took over from 616-536 B.C. Daniel said very clearly that he knew what he knew by studying the books written by Jeremiah. Why are you afraid to learn from somebody? Even a great man like Daniel was blessed by another prophet – Jeremiah.

In the first year of his reign, I Daniel understood by books the number of the years, whereof the word of the Lord came to Jeremiah the prophet, that he would accomplish seventy years in the desolations of Jerusalem.

Daniel 9:2

Open up your heart and become a learner and receiver. After all, we all learn from somewhere. **It is the insecure people who are afraid to show that they learnt what they know from somewhere!** Become so receptive that you receive the knowledge of the Word! Open your spirit so that you learn how to preach yourself! Open your heart so that you receive the anointing!

Levels of Receptivity

I want you to notice these levels of receptivity that I have listed below and ask yourself where you fit!

Level A: The Word has no impact. You do not understand the message. You probably did not even like the message.

Level B: The Word has an impact on you. You are excited and think that it is a good message. However, you only retain about eleven percent of what was preached. This is usually what happens when a person listens to a tape only once.

Level C: You absorb the Word even further but cannot reproduce the message.

Level D: You absorb the Word so much that you can reproduce the message.

Level E: You begin to learn how to preach and teach in the same anointed manner.

Level F: You absorb the Word and at the same time begin to absorb the anointing and Spirit of the message.

Level G: At this level, the transfer of an entire ministry gift takes place. Often an anointing which is on the speaker is transferred to you. Like John the Baptist and Elijah, similarities emerge between your ministries because the same anointing has been transferred.

Notice These Signs

These are signs that you are on the road to catching the anointing.

1. You are able to follow the trend of the message; even when it is confusing and disorderly.

2. You receive additional lessons that are not the main message. This is an important sign if you are catching the anointing on the minister. You begin to understand the mind and the heart of the person you are listening to. Most of these additional lessons you receive may be unrelated to the topic that is being taught. You begin to learn so many little things which may include a principled character, how to speak, how to analyze Scripture and how to overcome problems.

3. You unconsciously begin to use certain phrases and points in these messages. Unknown to you, you begin to walk and think like the person you are listening to.

4. You are able to minister the message with the same results. For instance church growth, miracles, people commenting that they were blessed, people buying your tapes and people wanting to hear part two and part three of your message. This is different from dry imitation, when you become an exact replicate of what you hear, but do not get the same results.

Avoid These Mistakes

I am not teaching you not to study the Bible for yourself. I am not teaching you to neglect personal Bible study. That is a great mistake! I am an avid listener of tapes but I study the Word of God everyday. **I have a personal quiet time every day. Many of my messages are what I have learnt from my daily Bible study**.

§   Avoid the mistake of not reading the Bible and doing Bible study for yourself.

§   Avoid the mistake of thinking that it is a man that is going to anoint you. It is God who anoints you through a man.

§   Avoid the mistake of only listening to tapes when you are going to preach. Listen to tapes all of the time whether you are going to preach or not. I listen to tapes all the time.

§   Avoid the mistake of not doing further study on subjects or tapes you listen to.

§   Avoid the mistake of preaching about things you do not practise. Do not preach about things that you do not understand or believe in (Ezra 7:10).

§   Avoid the mistake of simply imitating and copying someone without understanding the whole mystery of catching the anointing through soaking in the Word.

§   Avoid the mistake of leaving out the video dimension. The video dimension helps you to catch things that you cannot catch on an audio tape: posture, attire and gestures. Soaking in videotapes, helps you to learn how to minister the Spirit and to minister with signs and wonders.

Ignore the Ignoramuses

Listening to tapes over and over does not mean that you are engaging in mindless memorization. Some people call this, "chew and pour." I just laugh to myself when I hear such comments.

The most difficult time for me in the medical school was during the second year. During the second year we had to study physiology, anatomy and biochemistry.

Of these three subjects I found biochemistry the most difficult because it involved a lot of tedious memorization.

I am not teaching you to become a copycat. I am teaching you how to catch the anointing. I am teaching you to walk in the steps of anointed people. When a young girl is learning how to cook, she is taught to follow a simple routine. As she does this over and over, she is able to cook the food as well as her mother. With time she will develop her own variations and style. Would you call that daughter a mindless copycat? Would you say that she is engaging in senseless memorization? Certainly not! She is a humble learner.

What is a Clone?

Dear friend, the devil wants to keep you from the anointing. I have heard people speaking sarcastically about this method of catching the anointing. Someone once said that I was producing clones. What is a clone? Why do some people try to confuse God's sheep with clever sounding phrases? Quite frankly, I would rather hear my dogs bark in the morning than to listen to such stories!

When a doctor is learning to be a surgeon, he has to closely observe what his professor does. Then he assists his professor several times. Soon he gets an opportunity to do the procedure himself. He gingerly follows the procedure that he has seen his professor do. He may make a few mistakes, but soon he can perform the operation perfectly.

If you watch this new surgeon closely, you will realize that he is doing exactly what his professor does. With time, he develops his own additions or improvements to what he has learnt. Has the professor produced a clone? Certainly not! He has trained another competent surgeon.

When Paul was training Timothy for the ministry, he wrote to him and said, "My son preach the same things that I have preached to you. Spend time sharing the same things with the faithful brethren that you have."

Thou therefore, my son, be strong in the grace that is in Christ Jesus. And the things that thou hast heard of me among many witnesses, the same commit thou to faithful men, who shall be able to teach others also.

2 Timothy 2:1,2

Paul told Timothy to preach the same thing that he had preached. Was Paul producing a mindless clone? Watch out for people who try to re describe godly things and make them appear stupid.

When you "soak in" tapes many good things happen to you. You learn how to preach and you catch the anointing. It is funny how some people see things. Someone once said that he did not want to listen to tapes because he did not want to "lose his personality". How would you lose your personality by exposing yourself to the anointing and the influence that comes from special men of God?

When the choir in my church sings a song by Andrae Crouch or someone else, are you telling me that they have lost their personality? Do you know that they would have to rehearse the song for several hours in order to get it just right? As they soak in this music over and over and as they try to do exactly what they are hearing, are you telling me that they are losing their personalities? *As I said earlier, I prefer listening to my dogs bark in the morning to listening to such comments!* Remember what Paul said to the Corinthian Christians; he told them to follow him!

Be ye followers of me, even as I also am of Christ.

1 Corinthians 11:1

It is okay to follow people and to soak in their tapes as long as they are following Christ closely.

27

CHAPTER 7

"Aman" and "Tsalach"

> And they rose early in the morning, and went forth into the wilderness of Tekoa: and as they went forth, Jehoshaphat stood and said, Hear me, O Judah, and ye inhabitants of Jerusalem; Believe in the Lord your God, so shall ye be established; believe his prophets, so shall ye prosper.
>
> **2 Chronicles 20:20**

In this famous Scripture, you find Jehoshaphat, a church member, exhorting the rest of the congregation to believe in God as well as in the man of God. This famous speech teaches us a very great lesson for the ministry. In the first part of the Scripture, there is a prediction that believing in God will lead to establishment. In the second part of the Scripture, the promise is that believing in the prophet will lead to prosperity.

You see, Jehoshaphat was faced with a very difficult situation. Several kings were about to attack him and his nation was in crisis. He had called for a prayer meeting; much prayer had been offered to the Lord. At the end of the prayer meeting, one of the pastors (Reverend Jahaziel) gave a prophecy. He prophesied that they were going to win the war. He predicted that God was going to fight for them and that everything was going to be okay. Because of this, Jehosophat made the choir march in front of the army. That was a very dangerous move! But he believed in both God and the prophet – and it paid off! At the end of it all, Jehoshaphat and his followers had more blessings than they could carry away. God blessed them with more than they could carry!

And when Jehoshaphat and his people came to take away the spoil of them, they found among them in abundance both riches with the dead bodies, and precious jewels, which they stripped off for themselves, more than they could carry away: and they were three days in gathering of the spoil, it was so much.

2 Chronicles 20:25

The Hebrew word translated "established" in 2 Chronicles 20:20 is the word "Aman". It means "to nurture", "to foster as a parent", "to build up" and "to nurse". This teaches us that as you believe in God, you will be nurtured and nursed by God. He will build you up in the faith and you will receive a strong foundation that only a parent can give. But this Scripture goes on and says to believe in the prophets and you will "prosper".

The Hebrew word translated "prosper" is the word "Tsalach." It means "to push forward", "to go over", "to come mightily" and "to break out!" "Aman" and "Tsalach" are two very different experiences in the ministry.

God will nurture you and build you up for His work. He will nurse you like a baby in a cradle. He will foster you like a parent and encourage you until you are well developed. BUT THEN, YOU NEED A PUSH FORWARD IN THE MINISTRY.

You need to come mightily in ministry. You need to break out into the fullness of your calling. God wants you to go over every wall and obstacle in your life and ministry. The question is, *"How will you receive this push forward into ministry?"* After you have been nurtured and fostered by Almighty God, what is the key to coming mightily to the front of the ministry lines? **The key is to believe in the man of God**.

Some people have difficulty in believing in the man of God. They say, "I can believe in God, but I can't trust these men." They say, "I cannot put my trust in the arm of flesh." What you must realize is that you are not putting your trust in a human being, per se. The safety catch in this Scripture is that you are supposed to believe both in God and in the man of God. One without the other will not get you where you need to go.

Believing in God without believing in his prophets will help you to be nicely built up in Christ. But you will not have the push forward that you need. Believing in the man of God without believing in God is also very dangerous! You could easily make a mistake and follow the errors of a human being. That is why the two go together!

As you read this book, my prayer is that you would open yourself up to the blessings of "Tsalach". This is the blessing of being pushed forward mightily in the ministry.

My early Christian life was one of being nurtured by God through great fellowships like the Scripture Union. I was raised on the Word of God. I was nourished through both Bible studies and prayer. I can assure you that I grew steadily in the Lord.

As the years went by, I encountered men of God who had an impact on my life. Without realizing what I was doing, I began to follow ministers like Kenneth Hagin, Fred Price and David Yonggi Cho. I have closely followed and believed in the ministries and instructions of such men of God and it has pushed me forward in ministry. That is the reason why you are reading this book now!

I always have a book or a tape that I am "soaking in". It is alright to follow people closely as long as they are following Christ.

Be ye followers of me, even as I also am of Christ.

1 Corinthians 11:1

It is alright to believe in a man of God as long as you simultaneously believe in God.

God gives everybody a man of God. Through the man of God in your life, you will receive a push into ministry. You will catch the anointing and you will break out mightily. Do not make the mistake of rejecting the man of God that God gives to you.

The ministries of many people end up nowhere because they refuse to get connected to God through a man of God. In Ghana, we have the Akosombo Dam, built on the Volta lake (the world's largest man-made lake), as our major source of electricity. I can assure you that it generates a lot of power. If I want to get connected to that power, I do not have to travel to Akosombo. All I have to do is to plug into a nearby socket.

The socket nearby, is the man of God on this earth who you can relate with. By connecting to him you will be connecting to God who is 'far away' in Heaven. Plug into the socket and you will be connected to amazing power! Plug into the man of God and you will be startled to find that you are actually connected to incredible power itself. He that is plugged into the socket, is plugged into the Akosombo Dam itself.

Verily, verily, I say unto you, He that receiveth whomsoever I send receiveth me; and he that receiveth me receiveth him that sent me.

John 13:20

Look around and see all those "unimpressive" sockets around you. Look around you and see all the "unimpressive" men of God. Make a connection to God through his chosen vessels. You can do that by listening to their tapes, watching their video tapes and reading their books. Do not make the mistake of rejecting this great opportunity to be pushed forward in the ministry.

Jesus was rejected by the people of his hometown. They could not believe that this unimpressive carpenter was the man of God for their lives. When Jesus told them that he was anointed to heal and preach, they were offended and angry. They thrust him out of the city.

The Spirit of the Lord is upon me, because he hath anointed me to preach the gospel to the poor; he hath sent me to heal the brokenhearted, to preach deliverance to the captives, and recovering of sight to the blind, to set at liberty them that are bruised,

And all they in the synagogue, when they heard these things, were filled with wrath, And rose up, and thrust him out of the city, and led him unto the brow of the hill whereon their city was built, that they might cast him down headlong. But he, passing through the midst of them, went his way.

Luke 4:18,28-30

Others who believed in Jesus received him and were greatly blessed by his ministry. They received mighty breakthroughs for their lives and ministries.

When Peter, James and John began ministering in the Book of Acts, many people noticed that they were heavily anointed. They began to ask themselves, "Who are these young men who have *come mightily in ministry?*", "Who are these guys who have *pushed to the forefront* of ministry in Jerusalem?", "Where did they get an anointing to preach and to heal the sick?"

Now when they saw the boldness of Peter and John, and perceived that they were unlearned and ignorant men, they marvelled; and they took knowledge of them, that they had been with Jesus.

Acts 4:13

I see you being pushed forward in ministry! I see you coming mightily into the forefront of ministry in your city! I see you going over every obstacle and difficulty in your ministry! Tap into your man of God! "Soak in" the tapes and "soak in" the books! The anointing is yours for the taking! You are breaking out into fruitfulness and success in the ministry of the Lord Jesus Christ!

Heavenly Father, I pray for every young man and woman who desires the anointing of the Holy Spirit. I pray for every pastor in the ministry. I pray that you would open their eyes of understanding that they may see the truth that is in Your Holy Word. Pour out your power and your Spirit on the ministers of this end-time harvest. O Lord, we need your anointing more than ever before. As your people tap into the men of God that you have given to us, may a spirit of humility and receptivity engulf them. May precious mantles fall on those servants who desire to walk in a greater level of anointing. May every minister of the Lord Jesus who reads this book never be the same again! And may they be endowed with real power and real gifts from on high. Amen!

CHAPTER 8

Six Giants Catch the Anointing

I t is interesting to note how great men caught the anointing. Many people think that the anointing just comes to lucky people! In this chapter, I have presented the testimonies of six great men that many people know about. These people are not strangers to the Body of Christ. Most of us know the great things that the Lord has used these men to do.

The following testimonies are excerpts from books that have been written about them. These are not my words, I am trying to show you what they said about themselves.

Reinhard Bonnke and George Jeffreys

The following is an excerpt from a biography written on Reinhard Bonnke called '*A Passion for the Gospel*' by Colin Whittaker.

[1]*The train from Swansea took Reinhard Bonnke to London where he had a few hours to spare before the next stage of his journey to the overnight ferry. He was told the time-honoured way of seeing London was by the world famous, red London buses.*

Having enough money for a run-about ticket, he travelled the streets of the capital, changing buses at random. He was free, he was going home, and life and London looked wonderful from the top deck of a double-decker bus.

After an hour or two he needed exercise, so he alighted at the next stop and strolled down the road, with little idea where he was except that he was still within the bus routes of London. As he enjoyed the walk, a sign informed him that this area was called Clapham. The name meant nothing to him and he walked on until he found himself outside a house with a wooden fence around it and on it a board bearing the name, Principal George Jeffreys.

He stopped in his tracks and looked at the name again. It was there clear enough, but no; he dismissed it, it could not be.

Only a few weeks earlier, he had been browsing through the books in the college library when he chanced upon 'Healing Rays' by George Jeffreys. His interest was quickly aroused as he scanned through the contents.

It was a balanced scriptural exposition on the subject of divine healing. The final chapter was full of testimonies of miracles in the ministry of George Jeffreys which were witnessed by huge congregations in the largest halls throughout the British Isles. The founder and leader of the Elim Foursquare Gospel Alliance, he had clearly been a greatly anointed evangelist.

Reinhard had been absorbed, but he noted that the miracles mostly occurred in the 1920s. He presumed that this great evangelist must be dead, and when he had left college, George Jeffreys had been far from his thoughts.

But now he wondered. Was it possible that this great evangelist was still alive and lived here? He had almost decided that it was nonsense even to think so, when the Holy Spirit seemed to whisper in his heart, 'Why don't you find out?'

Contrary to what people may think when they see him in action on a platform, Reinhard is not one to rush into things; he likes to think before he acts. But at once he knew he must know the truth.

He went up to the front door and rang the bell. Just when he was beginning to think that there was no one in, a woman opened the door.

'Excuse me,' he asked, 'but I saw the nameplate and wondered is this the home of George Jeffreys the mighty evangelist who reached a whole nation?'

'Yes it is the same man,' she replied. 'Please, do you think that I may see him? I have just finished at Bible college and I am on my way home to Germany.'

Her reply was an unpromising 'No' and with that she started to close the door, when a voice echoed from within, 'Let him come in.'

In went the wondering Reinhard and there, coming down the stairs, was the frail figure of an elderly man. In a deep husky voice, he greeted Reinhard and asked him what he wanted. Reinhard explained how he had just finished Bible College and the call of God was on his life to be a missionary in Africa. He was led into one of the rooms, and invited to sit down. George Jeffreys sat down opposite him on a couch and began to ask Reinhard lots of questions about himself.

The fact that Reinhard had been at college in Wales helped to open the conversation with this Welsh preacher whose roots were in the Great Revival there in 1904, and the conversation ignited with the fire of a spiritual rapport which obliterated the generation gap. It was a meeting of two kindred souls with a mutual passion for evangelism. One who was reckoned by many to be the greatest British evangelist of this century, who knew he was coming to the end of his life. The other an eager young man who knew that God had given him the ministry of an evangelist, taking up the mantle of his ministry. Suddenly the old man slid onto his knees, pulling Reinhard down with him.

The glory of God came on Reinhard as George Jeffreys laid his hands upon his head and prayed for him. The tired but still eloquent voice gained in strength as the old Welsh revivalist poured out his soul in prayer for the raw and eager young man whom God had brought to his house for him to bless. He who had spent his life beseeching sinners to receive Christ was again seeking the face of God for the lost, but through the ministry of this young German kneeling with him.

Did God give George Jeffreys a glimpse into the future ministry of Reinhard Bonnke? Was he allowed a foresight of the tremendous expansion of the revival which was just at hand? We cannot know, but when Reinhard finally rose from his knees, he knew that he had received something powerful from God. He left the house 'dazed' at what had happened as the house-keeper closed the door behind him.

He could not take it all in. He had not even had George Jeffreys on his mind, yet in a city of around ten million people God had brought him to the man's door. The more he thought about it the more he thanked God for so leading him. He caught the night train for the Channel ferry and travelled back via Belgium to his home in Germany. Hermann and Meta were so glad to have their son home again and they all had much to talk about, but Reinhard did not mention his meeting with the great evangelist.

A few weeks later, Herman said, 'Reinhard, I have just received news that George Jeffreys, the famous evangelist, has died.'

Reinhard was stunned. 'That cannot be, surely? I saw him a few weeks ago on my way home.' Then he shared with his father the story of that wonderful meeting.

In the light of the great man's death the encounter was seen to be even more remarkable.

Twenty-five years later, in August 1986, Reinhard Bonnke conducted a campaign in Blantyre, Malawi, named after the birthplace in Scotland of David Livingstone, the great Africa missionary explorer.

God so owned the ministry of his servant that by the closing service, the crowds attending had grown to over 150,000. Later on in the year another campaign followed in Lilongwe, and again many thousands came to hear the gospel message. It was during this time that Reinhard was deeply moved by certain stirring words written by David Livingstone over a century before in 1853 when in that same region:

Future missionaries will be rewarded by conversions for every sermon. We are their pioneers and helpers. Let them not forget the watchmen of the night, we who worked when all was gloom and no evidence of success in the way of conversion cheered our path. They will doubtless have more light than we, but we served our Master earnestly and proclaimed the same gospel as they will do.

More than once as Reinhard blazed across Africa, the Holy Spirit reminded him of the immeasurable debt he owed to the many 'watchmen of the night' in whose steps he was treading. Most of them like Livingstone were long dead, but as Scripture says of Abel, they 'by faith still speak'. However, in the providence of God he had been allowed to meet one or two special watchmen of the twentieth century.

It was not until he was praying about the momentous decision to move the centre of his operations from Africa to Frankfurt in Germany that the Holy Spirit brought it very specially to his attention. Suddenly everything connected. God gave him a new realisation about how we build on the people who have gone on before us, those watchmen who faithfully carried the torch of truth in their generation, defied the darkness, and handed on the baton to those coming after who were ready to respond to the call of God; people such as David Livingstone, Rees Howells and George Jeffreys, and he knew that in some way God had helped him to grasp a baton. The greatness of the responsiblity weighed heavily upon him. He must not fail. The more he thought back over that meeting with George Jeffreys the more he realised how God had planned it; not only the amazing timing of it, so close to the end of the evangelist's life; not only as a German whose nation had been at war with Britain only a few years before; not only on the day he had finished at college; but also with one of the greatest evangelists of this century. God had confirmed his calling and this special experience seemed to cover him with an added mantling of his power.

Considering the incident under the direction of the Holy Sprit strengthened him and caused him to thank God for his guidance, but he was also enabled to keep it all in perspective. He knew that even the great George Jeffreys had made mistakes which had almost certainly limited his effectiveness in his later years. Nothing could ever detract from what the evangelist had achieved, but sadly he had become involved in a dispute over church government which had ultimately caused division in the Elim movement, and had also been taken up with another unprofitable diversion which led nowhere except to more controversy. It was a sombre lesson. If so great a man could make mistakes which marred his ministry, then what hopes for him? He prayed that God would continue to direct his paths and deliver him from ever being diverted from evangelism.

None of God's servants is superhuman, and Reinhard is aware that one day people may gloat over his mistakes also. We are what we are by the grace of God. An incident which could easily have puffed him up has served to keep him humbly aware of his need to watch and pray. The path of a successful evangelist is full of pitfalls.[1]

Kenneth Hagin and Smith Wigglesworth

The following is an excerpt from Kenneth E. Hagin's book '***Understanding the Anointing***'. Notice how the anointing flows from one great man to another.

[2]*Frequently, when some great man or woman of God passes off the scene like Elijah did, you will hear preachers say, "I wonder upon whom his mantle will fall?" We've all heard that said. But just because we've heard something said and have repeated it often doesn't make it so! Something isn't so just because we thought it so.*

I want you to see something here that can hinder you from entering into the blessings God wants you to have.

In 1947, I picked up a religious periodical and read that Smith Wigglesworth had gone to be with the Lord at age 87.

I felt a great loss. I remember I went into my church and fell across the altar. I didn't know the man personally but I had read about him constantly, actually wearing his books out, until something from him rubbed off on me.

You feel an emptiness - a vacuum - when a man of God of that caliber leaves - a man who had had 23 people raised from the dead in his ministry. People asked, "I wonder on whom his mantle will fall?"

In my ignorance, I, too thought that the mantle is the anointing, and it would fall at random on somebody. But that's not correct. The mantle symbolizes the anointing...

As we saw earlier, you get the same anointing by association, environment, and influence. No doubt you'll be led of the

Lord to follow certain ministries, but there are certain things that ministers need to be warned about in this regard. I'm in my 49th year of ministry. You stumble upon a few things in 49 years.

If you are going to follow somebody, be sure they are following the Lord. If they get off a little - just a little - don't follow that. Learn faith from them, but don't follow them too closely.

Remember these three things:

First, have the call of God on your life.

Second, follow the Lord Jesus - He's the Head of the Church - very, very closely.

Third, if you want the same type of ministry someone else has, follow that ministry closely.

If the desire for it is in your heart, it's usually because God put it there. But that mantle will not fall on you automatically, like ripe cherries off a tree.[2]

Benny Hinn and Kathryn Khulman

Benny Hinn is another example of someone who has caught the anointing. In his book *"Good Morning, Holy Spirit"*, he shares about how he received an impartation into his life through the ministry of Kathryn Khulman. He describes how he attended a Kathryn Khulman miracle service and how the Holy Spirit touched him at that meeting.

In Scripture, the similarities between the ministries of Elijah and Elisha were indicative of the similarity of the anointing on their lives. This is what gives us the authority to examine the similarities between different ministries today. Elisha asked for a double portion of the anointing that was on Elijah and he got it. Consequently, Elijah did sixteen miracles but Elisha performed thirty-two! Elisha performed exactly twice as many miracles as Elijah did and this is because he had a double portion of Elijah's anointing. The miracles of the two ministers were also similar. Both of them were involved in declaring famines in their communities. Both of them experienced the miracle of a young boy being resurrected from the dead. At one point in their ministry, Elijah and Elisha were both involved in drying up the River Jordan. Another important similarity is that they both gave accurate prophetic utterances, which came to pass.

My observation of the ministry of Benny Hinn leaves me with no doubt that he has indeed received something through the ministry of Kathryn Khulman. Simply put, I believe that Benny Hinn caught the anointing that was on Kathryn Khulman. There are many similarities between the ministries of Benny Hinn and Kathryn Khulman. These similarities are proof that the same kind of mantle which was on Kathryn Khulman is now on Benny Hinn.

The large crowds which gather at Benny Hinn's miracle services, are reminiscent of the kinds of audiences that Kathryn Khulman once drew.

The peculiar healing anointing that gives rise to all kinds of amazing miracles is also characteristic of both Benny Hinn and Kathryn Khulman. The unusual and tangible presence of the Holy Spirit that is experienced in Benny Hinn's services, is also a mark of the Kathryn Khulman anointing. The phenomenon of several people falling under the power during services is also a distinctive feature of both the Khulman and Hinn ministries. As I said, these similarities are proof that the same kind of mantle that was on Kathryn Khulman is now on Benny Hinn.

I am not sharing these things so that you sit back and say; "Wow, I wish I was Benny Hinn!" I am not sharing these things for you to marvel over the things great men of God have experienced. *I am trying to show you a principle that can work for you. You* can be anointed! *You* can catch an anointing! *You* can also receive great spiritual gifts if you understand the principles that govern the receiving of an anointing. The work is so much that God needs several anointed people to go forth with the Word. I do not believe that the anointing is for a special few. It is for you and me if we are prepared to pay the price!

T. L. Osborne and William Branham

The following is an interesting testimony about how T.L. Osborne caught the anointing. Notice how the anointing passed on from one great man to another.

[3]*The man who came closest to carving out a unique ministry during the early years of the revival was a young Oklahoma evangelist, Tommy L. Osborne. In the process, Osborne pioneered many new techniques for independent foreign evangelism and won the respect of most of his contemporary evangelists. When the revival declined in the late 1950s, many others, in efforts to survive, followed the trails Osborne blazed.*

One of thirteen children, Osborne was raised in the poverty of a depression farm in Oklahoma where he learned a deep trust in God. In 1937, when he was fourteen, he believed that God spoke to him and told him that he would preach.

Although he finished only the eighth grade, he became a minister in the small Pentecostal Church of God. In 1946, he spent a discouraging year in India as a missionary. He returned sick and disappointed and settled into a small local church in McMinnville, Oregon. At best Osborn's early years as a minister were a limited success.

In Oregon, a disillusioned Tommy L. Osborne awaited the fateful arrival of the William Branham party in the summer of 1947. On the first night of the Branham campaign in Portland, Osborne's wife was in the audience.

Daisy Osborne, a bright and forceful person in her own right, persuaded her husband to attend the next evening. Osborne later wrote:

As I watched Brother Branham minister to the sick, I was especially captivated by the deliverance of a little deaf-mute girl over whom he prayed thus: "Thou deaf and dumb spirit, I adjure thee in Jesus' name, leave the child," and when he snapped his fingers, the girl heard and spoke perfectly. When I witnessed this, there seemed to be a thousand voices speaking to me at once, all in one accord saying over and over, "You can do that."

Out of this experience "was born a unique missionary ministry that has reached tens of thousands for God."[3]

Bishop David Oyedepo and Archbishop Idahosa

Notice the testimony of Bishop David Oyedepo. He is a great man of God who is bearing much fruit in the Kingdom. This is his testimony in his own words.

[4]In 1987, I was watching a video programme dwelling on a message from Isaiah 53:1.

"Who hath believed our report? and to whom is the arm of the Lord revealed?"

My heart and eyes were glued to the programme. As I watched and listened to that crusade message, the power of God was hitting me so hard that I was in tears, there alone in my house! I went to bed in that state, and there was such a quickening in me.

I rose up early, went to the living room, and cried out, "God, show me the secret!" And in the midst of this experience, I heard a man walk in and put His hand on my back, and some waves went through my spine. I exploded in tears.

The following Sunday, as I stood up to preach in church and I said, "Let's welcome ourselves with this scripture...", and we opened to Psalm 110, before I could finish reading it, the power of God came down! There was no further preaching. There were all manner of healings!

All manner! And that gave rise to "Pentecost Flames", which was the stirring, devil-destroying invasion of Kaduna State (North of Nigeria).

Friends, the earlier you get exposed to this power, the better. There is power in Word encounter! Until you are a Word-lover you don't experience power. The genuine source of power is the Word.

Acts 10:44 records that, "While Peter yet spake these words, the Holy Ghost fell on all them which heard the word."

If you are into prayers for power and you also embrace the Word for the power, you'll never run dry.

As words are spoken, there is an impartation that takes place.

As prophetic utterances are made, there is an impartation that takes place.

In Ezekiel 2:2, prophet Ezekiel said, "And the spirit entered into me when he spake unto me..."

As you hear anointed words, don't only expect to get insight, expect to encounter impartation also.

In 1986, I was in a meeting in Tulsa, where Rev. Kenneth E. Hagin was ministering under the anointing of the Holy Spirit. I sat down somewhere afar off, and while he was speaking, I saw his face transfigured (I don't know how many people saw that), and there and then, I had an encounter. My heart exploded, and I began to sob openly. The Spirit entered into me and changed the entire course of my ministry!

Before then, I used to preach jumping all over the place and sweating.

But that day, the Spirit entered into me, and the serenity of Kenneth Hagin's style of ministration was imparted to me instantly!

When you present your heart as a tablet, you don't only receive insight, but you also receive an impartation that will enable the insight to produce.

"...no prophecy of the scripture is of any private interpretation... but holy men of God spake as they were moved by the Holy Ghost."

So when the Word is being spoken, you are not just encountering insights, you are also encountering the impartation of the Spirit that gathered it.

Don't make light anymore the time you spend listening to anointed teachers and preachers of the Word. As you listen and hear, don't only expect to receive insight, expect and prepare your heart to encounter the power of God as well.

Nothing is more authentic than that which comes direct from source.

"... for my mouth it had commanded, and his spirit it hath gathered them" Isaiah 34:16.

Many have encountered power through the spoken Word in many forms-audio and video tapes, television, radio, etc. People have encountered the baptism of fresh oil as they listened to the spoken Word.

Once I was watching Archbishop Benson Idahosa on a video tape and for the first time in my life, an unseen guest walked up to me. His footsteps were audible to me. And as he put his hands on my back, something went through me. That was when the anointing for miracles was released upon me. Ever since then, I see disease as fake and I see the ones who sympathize with it as ignorant. I see that you can be well if it is your desire to be well.[4]

John Osteen (Lakewood Church) and the Osbornes

John Osteen was the pastor of the Lakewood Church, one of the largest churches in the world. Notice what he said about listening to tapes. He didn't mind soaking in the tapes of other great men. All he wanted was to catch the anointing.

[5]*When you talk about Daisy, you talk about T.L. When you talk about T.L. you talk about Daisy. They are inseparable - always have been. Only heaven will record how many ministers are preaching the gospel today because of them.*
I feel so blessed to have known them both. When I first heard about the Osbornes, I read their book, "Healing the Sick and Casting Out Devils". I said, " I must find this couple." I wept when I saw the pictures of the multitudes and of the miracles. As a Baptist minister who had just received the baptism of the Holy Ghost, I had not believed that these things could happen in our day. I pondered: are these miracles real? Have I been left out?
I refused to quit until I got in touch with the Obsornes. They let me into their lives. I was determined to do something for my generation but I didn't know how to go about it.
But this woman and this man took me under their wings
and taught me how not to preach about Jesus but to preach JESUS.
Daisy and T.L. will have a part in all that we ever do at Lakewood Church to reach the nations of the world for Christ. They invited me to attend one of their crusades. They brought me to the platform to sit with them. They put their arms around me and let me look right into the faces of the people who had received miracles.

I mean, they made me stand right there and see those miracles, one after another.

T.L. and Daisy saw the hunger in my heart and they were determined that I should behold the glory of the Lord in action - right there before my eyes.

As I listened to their teaching, witnessed those miracles, and observed the simplicity of their ministry, I concluded, "This is scriptural. I can do this."

For the next eight years, I went all over the world, and God confirmed His word wherever I preached. Then He spoke to me to come back to Houston and build Lakewood Church as a great world outreach center - a base for reaching the nations with the message and love of Jesus.

Not long ago, Daisy did something very special for me. You may smile when I tell you what it was, but it was a kindness that I'll not forget.

I had been involved in Lakewood Church and responsibilities of pastoring. I had not been overseas to conduct a crusade for a long time. I had done it during those eight years, but then when God led me to build Lakewood Church as an "Oasis of Love in a Troubled World", I stayed in the USA and gave myself to pastoral ministry, with the exception of occasional missionary trips abroad.

We had decided to conduct a great gospel campaign and leaders' seminar at New Delhi, India, the capital of that enormous and historic nation. I was getting ready to go.

I had talked to Brother T.L. about it. I hadn't preached a crusade overseas in years and I had actually become frightened, wondering if I was up to the task. That may sound foolish, but it is true. I told T.L., "I think I have forgotten how to do it."

We had registered 3,200 pastors and preachers from all over India plus thousands of other leaders, workers and students. Although it may be hard to believe, I felt panic. So I called Daisy. I said, "Daisy, I'm getting on the plane tomorrow and I'm afraid I've forgotten how to preach." I said, "Would you FedEx me T.L.'s messages that he preached in your Hyderabad, India, crusade?"

*I said to her (with a smile inside, because she and T.L. know
me so well): "I'm telling you, if you don't send me those
tapes, I'm going to fail in that big crusade and seminar at
New Delhi. I don't know what to do. You've got to help me."
Of course, Sister Daisy laughed and said, "Pastor John, you
know how to preach." I said, "Sister Daisy, send me those
tapes or I'm a goner!" She assured me, " "You'll have them
in the morning, Pastor."
And she Federal Expressed to me the full set of T.L.'s preaching
tapes from their Hyderabad Crusade, sending them overnight
to Houston. I received them before leaving and I listened to
them all the way to India. And what works for T.L. and Daisy
works for John Osteen because it's the Word of God!
Daisy and T.L. have marked me and my precious wife, Dodie.
But not just us. Thousands upon thousands of preachers have
been blessed and uplifted by their godly influence.[5]*

The Principle Is the Same

What worked for these great and mighty men of God will
work for you. The principle of catching the anointing through
books and tapes is a time-tested and proven principle. It is time
for you to catch the anointing for yourself. You cannot continue
to minister with just a natural zeal. O what a difference will
come into your life when you are anointed!

Reinhard Bonnke is one of the greatest evangelists of all
time. His crusades typically draw crowds of anywhere up to half
a million people. How did it all begin? What is the secret of
this great ministry? It is the anointing that makes the difference!
Although Reinhard Bonnke's testimony is not about books or
tapes, the principle is the same— he caught an anointing! It
is the anointing that makes the difference! You must catch the
anointing. The anointing comes to people who desire it and who
go for it. Be it through laying on of hands or through soaking in
tapes, the principle is the same.

Soaking in the materials (books and tapes) of Smith
Wigglesworth worked for Kenneth Hagin. T.L. Osborne became

a great and world-wide evangelist after being blessed through the ministry of the Prophet Branham. The anointing has worked for John Osteen. John Osteen was not ashamed to soak in the tapes of T.L. Osborne. Bishop Oyedepo stated clearly how he was blessed by soaking in the videos and tapes of great men. This is how great ministries are born! This is how giants are made!

Dear friend, God is making you into another giant for his kingdom. Respect the anointing! Aim to get the anointing! The anointing makes the difference! Once you've known it, you will never be the same. Your ministry will never be the same!

CHAPTER 9

Why Some People Never Catch the Anointing

There are some people who never seem to catch the anointing. They may be near anointed men of God, but they just never seem to tap into that glorious anointing. In this chapter, I want to share with you, some reasons why certain people never become anointed.

When Jesus was on earth with us, he ministered under the power of the Holy Spirit. Somehow, there were some people who could never receive from him. They were cut off from the anointing by what I call 'human barriers' to the anointing.

And he went out from thence, and came into his own country... And when the sabbath day was come, he began to teach in the synagogue: and many hearing him were astonished, saying,

From whence hath this man these things? and what wisdom is this which is given unto him, that even such mighty works are wrought by his hands? Is not this the carpenter, the son of Mary, the brother of James, and Joses, and of Juda and Simon?

...And they were offended at him. But Jesus said unto them, A prophet is not without honour, but in

his own country... And he could there do no mighty work, save that he laid his hands upon a few sick folk, and healed them.

Mark 6:1-5

In this Scripture, you will notice that Jesus was not well received. He was actually made incapable of performing miracles! The anointing could not flow from him into others. He could not heal people, and people could not receive from him. In a similar way, there are people who cannot receive from some men of God. It is a universal problem which exists in even greater dimensions today. The gift of God walks about in our midst and we do not benefit from it!

Why were people unable to receive? Why could the anointing not flow into their lives?

The Barriers

There are several barriers that prevent people from receiving the anointing. These barriers are often the natural features and characteristics of the man of God. Any of these features could present a barrier that could keep you away from the anointing!

The names, sex, tribe and nationality of a person often present themselves as barriers to the anointing. Some people cannot receive from a man of God because of his family background. Just the mention of his family name puts them off. There are people who cannot receive from a woman. There are people who cannot receive from people of a certain tribe. There are Christians who cannot receive from people of other nationalities.

There are many Americans who would look down on a book written by an African. They wouldn't even look twice at the material! I have interacted with ministers of different nationalities. Just the mention of Africa turns them off! I have noticed that some Western Christians see Africans as beggars. No matter the gift of God in them, African pastors are often seen as 'hewers of wood, drawers of water, pushers of carts, and carriers of bags'!

This is unfortunate because God has anointed many Africans with gifts for the world. If you are the type of person who cannot receive from an African, you may be excluded from some great blessings!

One of the commonest barriers to receiving the anointing is the colour of the man's skin. Although God made all men equal, white people often cannot receive from black people. What I am saying is true and the proof of it is seen in churches all over America on Sunday mornings. Sunday morning is the most segregated time of the week! Black people flock to black churches pastored by black ministers. White people rarely go to churches pastored by black men and vice versa. Why is this? Once again the human barriers are at work. **The man of God may have what they need, but because it is packaged in the wrong colour, they will have nothing to do with it!**

What is the difference between a white man and a black man? Are we not all men? One thing which proves that we are all the same is the fact that you can transfuse blood from a White man to a black man without causing any problems! We are all '*homo sapiens*'. The only difference between the black man and the white man is the amount of the pigment *melanin* found in the skin. Why should the amount of *melanin* in my skin prevent you from receiving the anointing upon my ministry? Could it be that you will miss out on the will of God because of the amount of *melanin* in somebody's skin?

I have received many blessings in my life through people of different colours, race and tribe. I have been tremendously blessed by Ghanaian ministers and also by Americans. God has touched my life through black, white and yellow-skinned people. My life could have been very different if I had not opened up to all of these wonderful vessels.

I once asked someone "*What colour am I?*" He was a preacher who taught a lot on the "black man". I wanted to find out what category I fell into. You see, my late father was from Ghana and my mother is from Switzerland. Since I am a mixture, I wanted to know whether I was seen as a white person or a black person!

51

Unfortunately, this dear pastor placed me in one of these two categories. I wondered to myself why he insisted on putting me in one or the other, when I was actually half of each! Why do we want to categorize people? It is this categorization that becomes a barrier to receiving from a man of God.

What Is His Background?

The educational or family background of a person, his qualifications, his personal history (and rumours!) are some of the commonest barriers to receiving the anointing. Fortunately or unfortunately, God has decided to use human beings as vessels of his anointing. The human vessel will definitely have a background of some sort! This background may not be what you are used to. It may not be what you want! You may not like the tribe or family to which he belongs. You may not like the colour of his skin. But God will still use that human vessel. You see, God has many vessels and he uses whichever he wants.

But in a great house, there are not only vessels of gold and of silver, but also of wood and of earth; and some to honour, and some to dishonour.

2 Timothy 2:20

What about his age? Is the man of God old enough for you? Is he too young? Is he too old? In the secular world, people need to be a certain age to do certain jobs. Usually, you have to be over the age of forty to become the President/Prime Minister of a country. Because of such laws, people tend to think that anyone below the age of forty is not qualified to be a leader. This is unfortunate, because Jesus was only thirty when he began to minister. When the Levites in the Old Testament were thirty years old, they were considered old enough to minister.

From thirty years old and upward... shalt thou number them, everyone that entereth into the service, to do the work of the tabernacle of the congregation.

Numbers 4:30

Never forget that men's standards are not God's standards.

And he [Jesus] said unto them... God knoweth your hearts: for that which is highly esteemed among men is abomination in the sight of God.

Luke 16:15

Peter Received from Jesus

Now when they saw the boldness of Peter and John, and perceived that they were unlearned and ignorant men, they marvelled; and they took knowledge of them, that they had been with Jesus.

Acts 4:13

Most people quote this Scripture to affirm the fact that Peter received the anointing by associating with Christ. What you must realise is that Peter received Jesus in the right way. **Peter was very close to Christ and he could have become so familiar that he could no longer receive.** He could have taken the anointing for granted! He could have perceived Christ as a mere man with human frailties. Do you think that Christ did not have human frailties? The Bible says that Christ took upon himself our infirmities (frailties).

... Himself took our infirmities, and bare our sicknesses.

Matthew 8:17

Judas would never have betrayed Christ if he hadn't seen him as a mere man. Who would want to betray God himself?

One day, the Lord asked Peter, what people thought about him. Jesus did not ask those questions just to boost his ego! He was wondering how people were receiving his ministry.

... Whom do men say that I the Son of man am?

Matthew 16:13

He went on to ask Peter, *"What do you think about me?" "How do you see me?" "What is your opinion of me?"*

53

The way Peter perceived Christ was very important for Peter's future ministry. That is why the Lord asked Peter what he thought.

...But whom say ye that I am?

Matthew 16:15

Peter gave one of the most important answers of his entire life. He said, "I see you as a man of God; I see you as God's servant."

He continued, *"I see you as someone sent from God into my life. I see you as my deliverer and my saviour!"*

And Simon Peter answered and said, Thou art the Christ, the Son of the living God.

Matthew 16:16

Is that not interesting? After interacting with a man of God for so long, you can still receive him as an anointed vessel of God!

This is what the people of Jesus' home town were not able to do. Jesus came into his own country and preached the same type of message. He came with the same anointing and the same spiritual gifts. But the first response to Jesus was to question his background.

Is not this the carpenter, the Son of Mary, the brother of James, and Joses, and of Juda, and Simon? and are not his sisters here with us? And they were offended at him.

Mark 6:3

You should hear how people talk. Is the man educated? Is he from the right family? Does he have the right accent? By the way, how old is he? Which tribe is he from? Is he tall? What does he look like? What kind of personality does he have? Is he choleric or phlegmatic?

Can a Woman Do It?

I hear the minister is a woman! Can a woman deliver the goods? Surely a woman can never be as anointed as a man!

Please stop it right now! As they say in Ghana *"stop dat roff derr!"*

The most anointed healing minister I have ever known about was a *woman* — Kathryn Kuhlman. That woman carried a very strong healing anointing — yet she was not a man!

If the sex of the minister is so important to you, you may end up excluding yourself from much of God's blessing. God may desire to bless you through a woman. The essential difference between a man and a woman is found deep within the genes. Women have 'XX' genes and men have 'XY' genes. This is a very tiny difference.

Why should that little gene within, prevent you from receiving a life changing impartation?

Never allow any of these human elements to become pronounced in your perception of God's servants. They will just turn into barriers to the anointing.

What you must realise is that, we are like specks of dust before God. We are of no importance to him. He is not impressed by our human preferences and he has no intention of impressing us. If you are too choosy, God will bypass you and give his anointing to a humble person who can receive.

Who knows; maybe God may one day use you to minister to others. Why should anybody receive from a mere human like you if you were not prepared to receive from other human beings?

Drop all barriers right now! Open yourself to the Spirit of God! Receive the anointing of God as he blesses you through special human vessels! Do not let questions of age, sex, personality, colour, tribe, family background, education or even rumours block you off from the anointing!

Your life will never be the same when the barriers to the anointing are gone! These barriers are in your mind! They are psychological obstructions to the flow of God's gift. Humble yourself right now and receive an impartation of the anointing through a human vessel! ⁷⁷After all, you have no choice— that is the way the anointing flows!